YOU KNOW YOU'RE A SCROOGE WHEN . . .

by
Scott Matthews and Barbara Alpert

PINNACLE BOOKS

PINNACLE BOOKS are published by

Kensington Publishing Corp.
850 Third Avenue
New York, NY 10022

First Printing: November, 1996

10 9 8 7 6 5 4 3 2 1

Printed in the United States of America

YOU KNOW YOU'RE A
SCROOGE WHEN . . .

You persuade neighborhood kids the best way to make snow angels is facedown.

You sneak down Christmas morning and open everyone's gifts before they wake up.

You give jigsaw puzzles with missing pieces.

You drop Canadian pennies and Italian lira in the Christmas kettles.

You shop for gifts in the local drugstore on
Christmas Eve.

Everyone on your list is getting a *Flintstones: The Movie*
coffee mug.

You give your mailman the hideous tie Aunt Sadie sent
you last year.

You get your Christmas tree from the discard pile at
midnight on December 24.

You figure no one will notice your gifts are wrapped in used tin foil and old shoelaces.

You eat all the candy canes and popcorn off someone's tree without permission.

Your favorite Christmas movie is *Silent Night, Deadly Night.*

Your favorite Christmas window is the smoked meat display at the deli.

You sit on Santa's knee and whisper that all you want for Christmas is twenty-five extra pounds just like he has.

You think Tiny Tim was faking it.

You leave the price tag on your presents so people will know what they cost.

You know it's better to receive than to give.

You loved the scene in *Wall Street* when Michael Douglas proclaimed, "Greed is good."

You have a T-shirt that says, "Money *can* buy happiness."

You enjoy telling children "There is no Santa Claus."

Your favorite exercise is pinching pennies and squeezing the last dime from a buck.

Your Christmas card reads, "It's not the thought that counts—I expect a present."

Your Christmas cards are stamped with pilfered Christmas Seals.

You serve tiny cups of Jell-O pudding instead of a real Christmas pudding.

You give the environmentalists on your gift list a bag of soda cans to recycle.

You always walk bent over to look for change dropped
in the snow.

You bring home holiday road kill for your pets.

You keep the cards sent from Indian reservations and
never send a donation.

When you sing, *"It* came upon a midnight clear," you
always think Godzilla's in town.

You insist the bright star in the night sky is really a UFO convention.

You order the free books from book clubs, then change your address.

You have a party during the supermarket's free "Tasting Night" in the deli department.

You water down your own liquor.

You claim your house as a soup kitchen to get government surplus milk and cheese.

You fill your pockets with sugar packets whenever you eat out.

You have a fruitcake in circulation that you first received in 1958.

You call your parents 1-800-Collect on Christmas Day.

You know the complimentary hors d'oeurves menu of every place in town.

Your favorite Christmas carol is "I Saw Mommy Goosing Santa Claus."

You always collect money for Christmas caroling, but charity begins at your home.

You give your Christmas cookies piled in rinsed-out Chinese food containers.

You collect half-empty buckets of movie popcorn to string for your tree.

Instead of using cranberries, you string cherries you swiped from local bars.

You shellacked last year's leftover Christmas cookies to give as ornaments.

You love the beach at Christmas—and always bring your metal detector along.

Your snowman wears your neighbor's hubcap as a hat.

You like to sing, "Jingle bells, Santa smells . . ."

When a light goes out on your tree, you smile—and
don't replace it.

Your Christmas tip to the doorman: "Bet Rudolph at
Aqueduct in the eighth."

You return all your presents December 26 just to break the salespeople's hearts.

You don't give your employees the day after Christmas off.

Your idea of a Christmas bonus is a box of pencils bearing the company name.

You sprinkle sugar instead of salt on the ice in front of your house.

When you run out of eggnog, you serve tinted instant breakfast shakes.

You bring a can of pickled pig's feet to the food drive.

No matter whose name you get in the office grab bag, you give socks.

When you look at the Rockefeller Center tree, you always wish for a blackout.

Instead of "mulled" wine, you ask for some drink no one's thought about at all.

You send charity begging envelopes back empty, so they have to pay the postage.

You wrap half-empty cereal boxes and donate them to local toy drives.

You enjoy reminding people that "Santa" and "Satan" have the same letters.

You get your picture taken with Santa and use it for a dart board.

You decorate your windows with spray-on snow in the shape of killer avalanches.

You throw snowballs at the postman bringing yet another stack of holiday cards.

You recycle last year's cards as this year's holiday postcards.

You spread rumors Santa & Mrs. Claus are really Burl Ives and Martha Raye, reincarnated.

You believe Santa's workshop is a front for neo-Commies—after all, everything's RED!

You announce that Santa's elves are a bunch of whining wusses.

You think any reindeer named "Prancer" is a little light on his feet.

Within earshot of little kids, you announce that dinner—reindeer steaks—is served.

You add that the cherry on top of the Christmas pudding is really Rudolph's nose.

When you hear "Christmas" in a word association test, you say, "expletive deleted."

Your addition to a holiday grab bag is a photo of Richard Simmons as a skinny Santa.

You cover the windshields of neighbors' cars with spray-on snow.

You organize a petition drive to keep your block free of "tacky quasi-religious decor."

You rewrite " 'Twas the Night Before Christmas" so that creatures—creepy, crawly ones—are stirring all over the house.

Instead of candles in your windows, you light highway flares.

You agree to go Christmas caroling but you deliberately sing loud and off-key.

You tie jingle bells to the cat's tail.

You chuckle when people search through a box of tinsel for the gift *not* enclosed.

You drop missiles of mistletoe on unsuspecting friends.

You insist on picking apart your piece of mince pie to look for the meat.

You record a sarcastic dialogue tape to play while watching *It's a Wonderful Life.*

Your holiday card says, "It's un-American not to work on Christmas Day. . . ."

You stand in back at the Christmas pageant and yell "Author, author!"

Your idea of comfort and joy is *The Joy of Sex* by Alex Comfort and a half-empty bottle of Joy perfume.

You send for the record club free CDs, then mark the bill, "Deceased—return to sender."

You store your leftover barbed wire in the fireplace to discourage chimney invaders.

Your roof displays a neon sign:
REINDEER GO HOME.

You water your tree with Mountain Dew.

You tell your girlfriend's dad how much you admire his
"bowlful of jelly" when he laughs.

You write a letter to the editor suggesting the North Pole
as a future landfill site.

The next time someone tells you to "ask your angels,"
you tell them yours said No.

You always set your sled on a collision course for the
toboggan with the most riders.

You deliberately run out of food at your holiday party so
everyone will leave early.

You cut your orange juice with water tinted with
food coloring.

Your jacket features a button:
MISTLETOE HICKIES GLADLY PROVIDED.

You throw out your tree in February, and leave all the
fallen needles strewn in the hall.

You're giving your brothers and sisters each a bottle of
Florida swamp water.

You draw horns and black eyes on every Santa picture
you see.

29

You don't watch out.

You cry.

You pout.

You don't care what Santa's list says.

You'd rather be naughty than nice any day.

You spread kinky rumors about the reindeer games they wouldn't let Rudolph join in.

You pray for a foggy, rainy Christmas Eve.

You tell people outside churches the time of Midnight Mass has been changed.

You stuff your briefcase with rolls before leaving any restaurant.

You insist the song is really "The Third Noel."

You hold your thumb over the lens when you take holiday photos.

You ask everyone you know to fix you up with Christmas Carol.

You rearrange the furniture and animals whenever you spot a Nativity scene.

You annoy your colleagues by keeping a noisy partridge in a pear tree in your office.

When charity Santas ask you for donations, you retort, "Go sharpen your Claus!"

You only call friends with toll-free numbers.

You watch the Rockefeller Center ice skaters and yell, "Reinstate Tonya Harding!"

Instead of roast turkey, you're planning a Christmas Day wienie roast.

When you come to the table to carve the turkey, you're wearing a Jason mask.

You spike the eggnog with tequila this year.

When asked what you want for Christmas, you answer, "Howard Stern in Congress."

No one's making you wear any gay apparel—not this year, not ever.

You tie tinsel to your dog's tail.

You stomp on childrens' snow angels.

You paste a mustache on baby Jesus in the manger.

Each day you unscrew another bulb from your neighbor's outside Christmas lights.

You deck the halls with cows and collies.

You don't believe in Santa.

While pretending to admire the Toys for Tots display,
you sneak one into your bag.

You keep your chimney knee-deep in soot.

You pack your snowballs with ice.

When you pull off people's snow boots, you make sure
they tumble over.

You wrap recalled toys and donate them to
Toys for Tots.

You've never seen *It's a Wonderful Life.*

You throw water balloons at Christmas carolers.

You dress up like the ghost of Christmas past and scare kids.

You run over your neighbor's reindeer decoration, then push it aside as road kill.

You call elves Satan's little helpers.

Your yard features an abominable snowman ready to attack.

Under cover of darkness, you cut pine branches off your neighbor's tree.

You turn off the radio when someone's singing along to a Christmas carol.

You're planning to be a robber baron by next Christmas.

You promise to mail a child's letter to the North Pole . . . but you don't.

You challenge your nephew's snowman to a fight, and the snowman loses.

You use your snowblower to block your neighbor's driveway.

Your favorite phrase is "bah humbug!"

You snicker at other people's New Year's resolutions.

You always ask where a gift was purchased, so you can return it for credit.

You hand out pink slips on Christmas Eve.

You still answer the door by asking visitors, "What did you bring me?"

When you see someone standing under mistletoe, you run the other way.

You tie your neighbor's reindeer decoration spreadeagled to the hood of his car.

You know you're smarter than all three Wise Men put together.

Instead of putting coal in stockings, you fill them with coal dust.

You bite the heads off gingerbread men and leave the bodies behind.

You sit on and squash a child's paper chain.

You throw snowballs at the Salvation Army bell ringer.

You tie your bows with triple knots so no one can unfasten them.

You rummage through the Goodwill drop-off box to find your spring wardrobe.

You love putting snow down someone's back.

You speed through big slush puddles to splash pedestrians.

You keep unscrewing light bulbs from friends' Christmas trees.

You spike the eggnog with Vicks NyQuil to turn it holiday green.

You make a low-sodium salt lick for the deer.

You keep breaking ornaments "by mistake."

You can't stand to see anyone merry and bright.

You disturb the silent night by playing your music too loud.

You dream of baking laxatives into your Christmas cookies.

You tell a child to look along the side of the road for Santa's reindeer.

You deposit your "holey" underwear in the Goodwill box.

When anyone asks you for spare change, you say, "Bah humbug. Get a life."

Instead of good, you're rotten for rotten's sake.

You bake cookies in the shape of Santa in a swimsuit.

You give a child a toy requiring assembly—and refuse to assemble it.

You tell everyone you know what they're getting, then tell them the wrong thing.

You cheer for the Grinch when he steals Christmas.

When you play secret Santa, you do your best to offend or annoy.

You open all of the Advent calendar windows at once—and eat the candy.

You tell every overworked sales clerk that you want to send your packages home.

You hoard Christmas cookies and eat them in bed with the lights out.

You ask every Santa you meet if all that is padding, or just him.

You dip your hands in snow before shaking hands with relatives.

You keep changing your seat during Midnight Mass.

You donate your dented canned goods to a
local orphanage.

You tell your mother that she "ain't no Martha Stewart."

You get dirty slush all over your grandmother's
white carpet.

You give your boss a copy of *Working with
Difficult People.*

You tell your mail carrier you've just subscribed to two dozen new magazines.

You give your doctor a bill for the time he's kept you waiting over the past year.

You hang only broken candy canes on the tree.

You keep a big pair of shears handy to clip any angel's wings.

When you hear "Ho, ho, ho," you yell "Shut up already!"

You channel surf while others are trying to watch *Frosty the Snowman.*

You tell someone they'd look perfect as Santa with no extra padding.

You throw pennies into the tuba played by a member of the Salvation Army band.

You leave skim milk and reduced-fat cookies on the mantel for Santa.

You tell a child that Santa Claus and Mrs. Claus are getting divorced.

You make up nasty new words to "Oh, Come All Ye Faithful."

You take one bite out of each of the Christmas cookies.

You make fun of anyone wearing red or green.

You fill the paperboy's Christmas envelope with a card saying, "Maybe next year."

You tie knots in all the empty stockings.

You hiss your way through a performance of Dickens' "A Christmas Carol."

You refuse to get out of bed on Christmas morning,
even when your children beg.

You give your significant other something insignificant.

Your idea of a great Christmas dinner is a McDonald's
Extra-Value meal.

You give last year's fruitcakes as doorstops this year.

You think mistletoe is something that astronauts get.

You consider Ebenezer Scrooge and Jacob Marley your true role models.

You think Bob Cratchit was a whiner.

You start seeing ghosts of the past, present, and future.

You would have returned the Magi's gifts—who needs myrrh?

You post a fat gram chart next to a basket of Christmas butter cookies.

Your rotten disposition never takes a holiday.

You yell "Merry Xmas" as you cut off a car to get the last parking space in the mall.

You like to sing, "We wish you a rotten Christmas."

You secretly hope that no one's Christmas wishes come true.

You berate a sales clerk who's too busy chatting to wrap your gift swiftly.

You think the holiday blues are a lovely color.

You insist on playing with a child's electric train set before he can take a turn.

You wrap up your unused Aramis gift set and donate it to Toys for Tots.

You lead a group of carolers in bawdy Christmas carols at a home for the elderly.

Even though some friends are alone for the holidays, you don't invite them over.

You mail a child's letter to Santa without postage so that it's Returned to Sender.

You look for reasons to be miserable and ruin other people's Christmas.

You bump into a person overburdened with bags, and you don't stop to help.

You begin your thank-you notes with "I enjoyed returning your gift . . ."

You avoid ringing bells so no angels can get their wings.

You shop for a super-tacky secret Santa gift, preferably a whoopie cushion.

Your note from Santa to a child begins: "My list says you have been very bad . . ."

Your favorite cartoon character is Scrooge McDuck.

You sideswipe another car into a snowbank.

You convince a youngster to lick an icy metal pole.

Every night you ask yourself what you did to ruin someone's holiday today.

You order some ugly holiday gift from a home shopping network, and send it C.O.D.

You'd rather watch a playoff game than go to see *The Nutcracker* with your kids.

To keep skaters away, you hang the "WARNING: THIN ICE" sign every day.

When you see people get splashed with slush, you can't help but smile.

You give your best friend a copy of *How to Be Your Own Best Friend.*

You send out postcards that say, "Christmas is cancelled this year."

You invite some grunge rockers to sing at a senior citizens' center.

You agree with the Church Lady about whose fault
Christmas is—could it be *Satan?*

You give your favorite Santa some Ultra Slim•Fast and
Tommy Lasorda's number.

You give empty bottles labeled "Fresh Air" as gifts
this year.

You tell someone who gives you something for your
hobby that you've given it up.

You can't bring yourself to celebrate any day that's also Barbara Mandrell's birthday.

You give cubic zirconium jewelry and pretend it's real diamonds.

You tell someone waiting under the mistletoe you'll be right back, promise.

You shake up your gift tins of cookies, just to be sure that lots will break.

Before giving a gift of chocolate Santas, you let them melt for a few hours.

You always dump your current lover before Christmas to save the cost of a gift.

You weren't convinced by Jimmy Stewart that it is, in fact, a wonderful life.

You start your Christmas shopping December 26—when everything's on sale.

You tell dirty jokes about shepherds in fields where they lay with their sheep.

You secretly trim the antlers off a neighbor's reindeer display.

You don't know what a noel is.

You suspect the three Wise Men were the forerunners to today's wiseguys.

You don't believe in miracles on 34th Street, or anywhere else.

Your thank-you notes arrive in June, if at all.

You start to count your blessings and can't get past zero.

Your heart races and eyes twinkle when you hear, "Attention Kmart shoppers."

You don't believe in giving sleighs the right of way.

You speed through "REINDEER CROSSING" zones.

You don't brake for elves.

You call 911 when you hear a clatter of tiny hooves on the roof.

Visions of sugar futures dance in your head.

You'd never spring for sugarplums at *these* prices!

You don't return holiday phone calls until the rates go down.

You give a constant dieter a scale that screams "You're fat!"

You don't have any Friends and Family.

"Interesting" is the best you can say when praising people's holiday decorations.

You stuff the Christmas goose with last year's leftovers.

You burn the roasted chestnuts but still expect your guests not to waste them.

You tell a child that Santa's home melted because of global warming.

You suggest people start their diets on Christmas Day.

You sew costumes for a children's Christmas pageant from itchy flour sacks.

You refuse to hint for gifts, then hate what you get.

You tell a child that an earthquake destroyed his snow fort during the night.

All you offer Christmas carolers is packets of cocoa mix to make at home.

You tell the kids on Christmas morning that Christmas has been cancelled.

You fill your cat's stocking with old catnip toys and silenced squeaky toys.

You fill your guest bathrooms with holiday toilet paper that turns the bowl green.

You sleep through the first grade Christmas play.

You criticize everyone's Christmas gifts, giving most a thumbs down.

You bring tidings of discomfort and misery.

You make your poor dog wear antlers.

You decorate your wreath with black-sprayed
holly berries.

You have been diagnosed by a professional as
"generosity-challenged."

You fax the President about the high cost of keeping
the National Christmas Tree lit.

You make origami dollar signs to decorate your
Christmas tree.

You hang Beavis and Butthead ornaments on your tree.

You think Christmas is Santa's ruse to get out of the house without Mrs. Claus.

You believe Christmas is a scam by big corporations to sell greeting cards and toys.

You eat an entire box of chocolate cherries rather than share them with others.

You give library books as Christmas gifts.

You consider the holidays a perfect time to make some new enemies.

You give each relative a locked bank to save their pennies—and you keep the key.

You spot an empty bird feeder, and think it will burn well in your fireplace.

You believe New Year's resolutions—except to save more—are made to be broken.

Forced to read " 'Twas the Night Before Christmas," you omit the dull parts.

You give such big hints, there are no Christmas morning surprises left.

You won't waste the gas to stop for stranded motorists standing in the cold.

You give free government booklets and Post Office Mover's Guides as gifts.

You say, "I gave at the office" when charities call—even though you really haven't.

You kiss people under the mistletoe, even when you know you've got the flu.

You exaggerate at least four times the price when you admit what a gift cost.

When someone opens your chintzy present, you don't even feel embarrassed.

You tell a Santa who has been standing in a store all day that he needs Right Guard.

You buy your gifts last-minute from the 7-Eleven on Christmas morning.

You mail your Christmas cards without a return address or postage.

You give piles of coupons clipped from the
Sunday paper.

You always wish the holidays were over before
they begin.

You leave the chimney flue closed when you light a fire
to smoke out your in-laws.

You'd rather listen to Muzak Christmas carols than a
choir of cute five-year-olds.

You'd rather do anything else on Christmas morning
than spend it with the family.

You give a balding person a gift certificate to the Hair
Club for Men.

You've been heard to utter, "Christmas sucks!"

Your bank balance is higher after Christmas
than before.

You fill stockings with Tums when a certain someone is making Christmas dinner.

You give your nicest presents to your banker, your broker, and yourself.

You're glad that Christmas specials get such low ratings they've been cancelled.

You duck down in your seat when a movie ends so you can slip into another one.

You schedule an urgent company meeting on
December 24—no absences accepted.

You still drive a VW beetle from the sixties that all your
friends call the "Humbug."

Instead of buying gift boxes, you use discards from the
supermarket.

You can burp out the refrain to "The Twelve Days of
Christmas."

You give a velvet, glow-in-the-dark Elvis painting to a classical music lover.

You give your annoying nephew an ant farm without any ants.

You give a copy of *Final Exit* to a relative in a nursing home.

You serve minnow flambé for Christmas dinner.

You'd never go from store to store to find a child the only White Power Ranger.

Your favorite book is *Cold Cold Heart.*

You'd be happy to give someone their "two front teeth" for Christmas.

You give your old eight-track tapes, telling everyone they're coming back.

You recycle the envelopes from the cards you receive
by steaming them open.

You serve turkey-shaped Spam out of the can for
Christmas dinner.

You check out all the Christmas books from the library
and keep them until March.

Your hero is Newt Gingrich—at last there's a Grinch in
Congress.

You mail your least favorite aunt a gift box full of Styrofoam peanuts.

You deliberately forget to include the batteries in a child's gift.

You fill someone's stocking with used car air fresheners.

Your stocking stuffers come out of gumball machines.

You bag freshly dropped manure and give it to a gardening enthusiast.

Your travel buff cousin gets a gift certificate for a night's stay at a Motel 6.

You ask your boss if you can work on Christmas Day at triple overtime.

You think the boxes of pens you pilfered from the office will make great gifts.

You post a "CURB YOUR REINDEER" sign on your roof.

You write B.Y.O.B. on your Christmas party invitations.

You revive the Pet Rock fad by giving boxed rocks from your backyard.

You hide snowballs in the nearest pair of boots.

You think Chia Pets and Soap on a Rope make great
stocking stuffers.

You drop fizzies in white grape juice and pass it off as
expensive champagne.

Instead of Eau de Toilette, you give bottles of
the real thing.

You give your wife an iron so old it doesn't
provide steam.

You give your husband a television set so outdated it
lacks a remote control.

You wouldn't mind if Santa showed up missing
—and on the back of a milk carton.

Books by Scott Matthews and Barbara Alpert

Santa's Little Instruction Book

How To Be A Christmas Angel

You Know You're A Scrooge When . . .